C000243785

WESTBURY

IN OLD PHOTOGRAPHS

THE COMMON SEAL OF WESTBURY. The actual seal was destroyed in a fire in 1935. It was of silver 1⅝in. across. The legend around the shield reads: 'SIGILLVM * MAYORIS * ET * BVRGEN * DE * WESTBVRIE'. The ivory handle was inscribed: 'MATHEVS * LEY * HOC * DEDIT * Aº * DM 1597 +'.

WESTBURY
IN OLD PHOTOGRAPHS

COLLECTED BY
MICHAEL RANDALL

ALAN SUTTON
1988
Published in collaboration with

Wiltshire County Council
Library & Museum Service

Alan Sutton Publishing Limited
Brunswick Road · Gloucester

First published 1988

British Library Cataloguing in Publication Data

Westbury in old photographs.
1.   Wiltshire. Westbury, history
I. Randall, Michael
942.3'15

ISBN 0-86299-524-8

Front Cover Illustration:
Shepherd with his sheep below the White Horse in 1905.

Typesetting and origination by
Alan Sutton Publishing Limited.
Printed in Great Britain by
WBC Print Limited.

CONTENTS

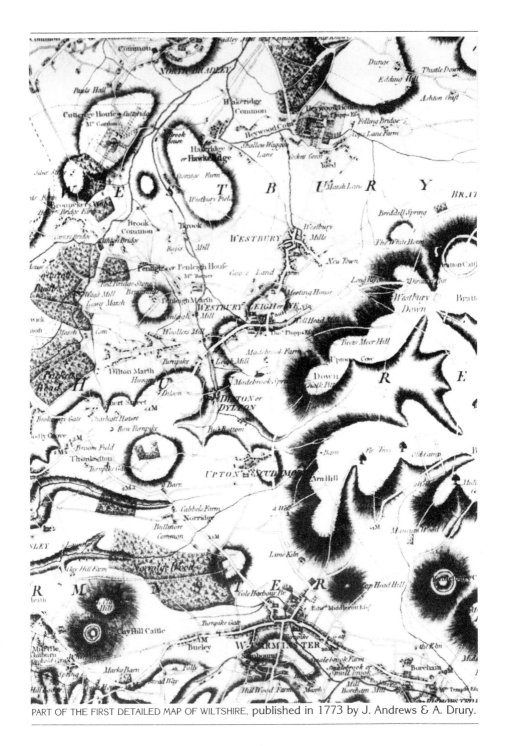

PART OF THE FIRST DETAILED MAP OF WILTSHIRE, published in 1773 by J. Andrews & A. Drury.

INTRODUCTION

Of the many Westburys, the Wiltshire one stands out for its proximity to one of the best-known White Horses, which is cut into the chalk on the western scarp of Salisbury Plain. The name was given by the Saxons after the Romans left Britain and means 'the fortified place in the west'. It appeared in the Domesday Book of 1086 as 'Westburie' and was the only manor in 'Wiltunscire' to have beekeepers listed, which perhaps indicates that agriculture thrived here in Saxon times. It is a pity the more distinctive and charming 'Westburye-under-ye-Plane', as described on Saxton's map of 1576, was not perpetuated.

A considerable collection of Roman artefacts was found on The Ham and, more recently, at Wellhead, Chalford and Chalcot, so there must have been a significant Romano-British settlement here from the first to the fifth centuries. The Romans mined iron ore on The Ham within a few years of their landing in AD 43. Unfortunately there appears to be no record of their name for Westbury.

Traces are clearly visible of the earlier inhabitants who made their settlements on the downs above the wooded and less safe vale. In the area of Bratton Castle, immediately above the White Horse, there is a Neolithic long barrow of c. 3500 BC and round barrows dating from the Bronze Age between 2000 and 500 BC. The earthworks of the Iron Age 'castle' itself were begun before 100 BC and fields were cultivated. Gradually, as agriculture developed and the woollen industry grew, the site of Westbury just below the Plain would have been attractive with its plentiful water supply from springs below the chalk.

During the late seventh or eighth century the villages of Bratton, Westbury, Chalford, Westbury Leigh and The Ham were grouped into the Hundred of Westbury – an area which would therefore have contained about 100 families. In the ninth century the first church was built on the site of the present fine medieval church of All Saints and the parish extended over the same area as the hundred. Bratton became a separate parish in 1894 as did Dilton Marsh which had grown up later, separate from Dilton, or Old Dilton as it is now known.

Wool and cloth making was the basis of prosperity in Westbury for over 600 years passing through recessions and recoveries – the last cloth mill not closing until 1967. Despite the general decline in the nineteenth century, when tanning, leather and glovemaking largely took over, the enterprise of Abraham Laverton and his son William made the Laverton Cloth Company successful and the town has benefited from their prosperity. Many reminders of their beneficence remain today.

The rediscovery of iron on The Ham in 1841, when the railway was being cut, gave rise to the Westbury Iron Works alongside the station. The company struggled against various economic pressures, was bought out by the New Westbury Iron Works in 1903 and finally gave up smelting in 1923. Its operations producing iron oxide and slag-based road surfacing tapered off and the plant was sold before the Second World War.

The railway put Westbury on the map when, early this century, the Great Western Railway ran its main West Country expresses on the shorter 'Westbury Route' to Exeter, Plymouth and Penzance. From a seat on the 'Cornish Riviera' or 'Torbay Express', hauled by a splendid 'King' or 'Castle', many a traveller will have known Westbury only from the excellent view of the White Horse seen out of the window. I had that pleasure nearly 40 years ago, but my destination was Westbury to be put through my paces at the Regular Commissions Board! Little did I think then that I would make my home here a quarter of a century later.

The town is now expanding so rapidly that we are in danger of losing sight of our heritage. I hope this book will give some nostalgic pleasure to those who have roots in an earlier Westbury and a greater feeling of belonging to a long established community to those who, like me, have chosen to live here in more recent years. It is not meant to suggest that everything that is old is good but perhaps it will help to identify what is good both from the past and the present. Let us hang onto that while endeavouring to make things better for those who come after, without letting purely commerical pressures dictate the progression of an urban jungle.

Without further ado, we will wander through the streets of Westbury in our imaginations and stop to glimpse frozen moments from the time of Queen Victoria to that of Queen Elizabeth II.

The Parish Church of All Saints

The church stands in its walled churchyard, changed but little in character over the centuries. Though alterations, repairs and restorations have been made throughout its existence, no records have survived for these before the nineteenth century. Some of the alterations made over the last 150 years can be seen in the photographs. Funds, as ever, are still needed to ensure the building is passed on to future generations in sound condition.

It is a good place to start our wander through the town of yesteryear for there is a reference in the Domesday Book (1086) to a church, so there must have been a Saxon structure of which no trace remains. Perhaps it was this church that was given by Henry I to Salisbury Cathedral c. 1110, for no reference to a Norman building has been found. However, the cruciform plan of the present mid-fourteenth-century church is typically Norman, so it is possible the foundations of an older Norman church were used.

These foundations began to move in 1968 when water leaked in, softening the clay subsoil which caused the tower to lean dangerously to the west. Stabilization was achieved in 1969 by sinking 137 steel piles 55 ft. into the ground to support concrete rafts around the base of the pillars. These were linked together to form a load-bearing framework.

'Pigot's Directory' of 1822 described the church as a 'neat and venerable pile' whereas 'Kelly's' of 1867 says it was a 'very beautiful building, with a fine large tower, in the Perpendicular style' and in 1899 more prosaically as; 'a building of stone ....'. Whatever its description, we are fortunate to have such a fine example of a medieval church.

VICTORIAN ENGRAVING made after Abraham Laverton had donated stained glass for the great west window in 1868.

AN EARLY TWENTIETH-CENTURY PHOTOGRAPH which can only be dated by the lack of yew trees by the west door.

INTERIOR VIEWS from the early nineteenth century after the nave had been re-roofed and the chancel given a new plaster ceiling. Note the box pews, the style and position of the pulpit and the absence of stained glass. A three manual organ, built by G.P. England in 1814, was installed in a gallery on the west wall. In 1866 Henry Bevington built a new organ which incorporated some parts of the old one. It can be seen on the next page. In 1888 Bevington was asked to place the console on the north side of the chancel which he achieved by turning the organ itself through 90° in the opposite direction. This relatively untouched fine Bevington organ is still in use, though feeling its age.

AN ENGRAVING FROM THE LATE NINETEENTH CENTURY. The present pulpit is in position, the font moved and plaster ceiling removed.

All Saints Westbury Parochial Accounts from Easter 1882 to Easter 1883.

1882 Offertories and Receipts	£·s·d	£·s·d	Expenditure	£·s·d
Balance from last years account		7·5	Organists Salary	15·0·0
April - Offertories for Church Expenses	10·2·11		Sexton's - -	25·0·0
May	9·2·11		As clerk to Funerals	2·10·0
June -	10·9·3		Organ Blower	2·0·0
July	10·2·2		Gas	19·0·11
August · · . . .	11·5·3		Fuel and cartage of ditto	10·17·8
September -	6·6·0		Lighting and maintaining fires	1·15·0
October - - - . . .	12·10·0		Visitation fees and Expenses	1·10·6
November · . · . . .	7·15·4		Messrs Bevington, Tuning & repairing Organ	16·10·0
December · · · . . .	9·16·8		Insurance	1·0·0
January 1883 · · · . . .	9·13·2		Laundress	6·1·0
February ·	8·19·7		Cutting grass in Churchyard	1·11·4
March ·	5·5·2		Mr Michael. Stationery	7·0
		111·7·3	Sundry small accounts	8·0
Subscriptions- The Iron Company	5·0·0		Offertories received by Vicar for:-	
Messrs Cockey	1·0·0		Sick and Poor	11·14·0
Offertories for - Sick and Poor	11·14·0		Widows	6·9·5
Widows	6·9·5		Diocesan Societies	14·7·4
Diocesan Societies [2yrs]	14·7·4		Hospitals	8·6·1
Hospitals	8·6·1		Decorations	5·5·1
Decorations	5·5·1		S. P. G. Society	8·13·2
S.P.G. Society	8·13·2		Alton Fund	1·4·8
Alton Fund	1·4·8		Choral Association	6·16·7
Choral Association	6·16·7		House of Mercy	10·7
House of Mercy. Salisbury	10·7		C. of E. Working Men's Society	9·5
C. of E. Working Men's Society	9·5		National Schools	5·8·6
Schools	5·8·6		Balance in hand	4·8·3
		£186·19·6		£186·19·6

Examined and passed in Vestry. March 29th 1883. Walter Butt. Vicar

AN INTERIOR VIEW SHOWING THE OAK ROOD SCREEN, installed in 1914 in memory of Mrs Kaye. The tiled floor was laid in 1867.

THE CHURCH HAS NOT CHANGED MUCH SINCE THIS WAS TAKEN, though the fifteenth-century font has moved twice since. The screen has gone, though the rood beam remains. It is in shadow here.

ALL SAINTS CHURCH CHOIR in 1925. Front row (seated): Parsons, -?-, Cutler, Revd Alexander, -?-, Burgess, Seaward. Centre row: -?-, Jones, -?-, -?-, -?-, Holloway, -?-, -?-, -?-, Jefferies, -?-, -?-, -?-, -?-, -?-, -?-, -?-. Back row: Hart (Verger), -?-, Gowan, Jones, Holloway, Edis, -?-, -?-, -?-, -?-.

LADIES OF ALL SAINTS CHOIR C. 1930. Front row: -?-, Mrs Richards (née Alexander), Revd Mock, Revd Alexander, -?-, Miss Alexander, Miss Webb (later Mrs Holloway). Middle row: -?-, -?-, Miss Gale, -?-, Miss Scull. Back row: -?-, -?-, Miss Gale.

THE ORIGINAL RING OF SIX BELLS on the ground after the ancient oak frame was found to be unsafe in 1920. The oldest bell was given by Sir James Ley of Heywood in 1616. Others were added in 1620, 1671, 1738 and 1741.

TWO SMALL BELLS were added when the six were recast at Taylor's of Loughborough in 1921. All the original inscriptions were reproduced. It is now the third heaviest peal of eight in the world. All eight bells were rung at once to test the strength of the new foundations in 1969.

CHOIR AND BELLRINGERS OUTING, 1920, in front of the Crimean cannon. Standing in front: Bill Say, Mr Edis, Canon Clarke, Bert Scull (driver). Others identified are: Messrs Hart (verger), Pidding, Cutler, Parsons, Jip Jefferies, Parsons, the Woodward brothers, Perrett, Seaward, Burgess.

A CHURCH OUTING IN MARKET PLACE in 1925. Alfred Street is in the background. Mrs O. Parsons is standing on the left and Revd Alexander is in the centre. The driver is Mr Slade. Others identified are: Mrs Parsons with her daughters Violet, Ethel and Evelyn, Lillian Blake, Mrs Gowan (standing behind the driver), Amy Hart, Phyllis Horler and Nellie Scull.

MODEL T FORD 'CHARA' opposite the Co-op with Fore Street in the background. 'Ginger' Brown is the driver.

BELOW THE BONNET ON THE AEC CHARABANC is painted 'Max Speed 12 mph'. The ladies' hats are no doubt firmly skewered with hatpins to withstand this reckless pace.

THE CHURCH GARDEN FÊTE. Shown in the picture are: Mrs Argent, Mrs Elliot, Mrs J. Francis (mother of Mrs Argent), Miss M. Elliot and Master K. Francis.

THE REVEREND STAFFORD BROWN, who did a great deal for All Saints Church and the town, unfortunately sold the unusual 1½ lb. silver-gilt Acorn Cup in 1845 to raise money to buy new plate, not realising its great rarity. The cup is hallmarked 1585 and was given to the church in 1671 by Mary, Countess of Marlborough. After changing hands several times, the cup is now in the Fine Arts Museum of Boston in America. The only comparable vessel is a gold Acorn Cup from Leicester in the British Museum.

REPAIRS in 1969. Interlinked 'rafts' under the pillars.

A SERVICE HELD AMIDST THE REPAIRS.

The Market Place

We leave behind the peace and feeling of permanence of the churchyard and enter the market place which presents an air of mature grace, marred today by the clutter of parked cars.

The right to hold a weekly market was granted in 1252 by Royal Charter. A market is still held in Westbury but it no longer takes place in the Market Place. No buildings of that age remain but the coaching inn has fourteenth-century origins. When the lord of the manor was the Earl of Abingdon, that was the name of the inn. It was changed in 1800 when Sir Mannasseh Massey Lopes bought the manor. In 1815 he built the Market House which was later used as the Town Hall and, for a while, housed the public library. It was said to be given as a peace offering to the town after an election scandal.

The Russian cannon from the Crimean War was melted down to aid the war effort in 1940, though its site remains Cannon Green.

The church tower is visible over the rooftops and, facing the square at the other end, is the elegant Queen Anne frontage of Marlborough House. James Ley, who later became the Earl of Marlborough, bought property in Westbury in 1600. This town house was probably built by a descendant around 1700.

THE MARKET PLACE at the turn of the century. The Russian cannon came from the Crimean War but was taken for scrap metal at the beginning of the Second World War. Marlborough House faces the square in the background. Gas lighting was installed in 1872.

Town Hall and Russian Gun. Westbury.

INQUISITIVE CHILDREN peer through the hedge which has grown since the previous picture was taken.

NOTE THE THREE-WHEELED 'VELOCIPEDE' IN THE CENTRE. The entrance to the churchyard is past the Lopes Arms in the background. A photograph taken in the 1890s.

HORSE ARTILLERY attracts a crowd at about the same date.

A VIEW FROM THE CHURCH TOWER in 1950. The gasholder in the background was dismantled in 1988. The weighbridge can be seen in front of the Market House.

THE FIRST WORLD WAR MEMORIAL. Bitham Mill chimney is visible over the roof of the Lopes Arms.

ARTHUR SCULL of Cannon Green.

EDWARD SCULL,
POSTING HOUSE, MARKET PLACE, WESTBURY, WILTS.

SOCIABLES, ⋄ BREAKS, ⋄ FLYS, ⋄ AND ⋄ BROUGHAMS,
FOR HIRE AT MODERATE CHARGES.

WEDDING & PICNIC PARTIES ON SPECIAL TERMS.

OPEN FUNERAL CAR. The Funeral Department promptly attended to & on reasonable terms.

THE SCULLS have provided transport in Westbury for generations and they still do.

THE MARKET PLACE is the focal point for many events. The poster for Queen Victoria's Golden Jubilee announces that the Band of the Westbury Company of the 1st Wilts Rifle Volunteers will play from 11 o'clock and the Assembly will sing the National Anthem there before the procession moves off at 3 o'clock.

MANY YEARS LATER the band, under Bandmaster Charles Bailey, arrives with its horse transport outside the Crown Hotel.

LILY TUCKER leaving the Crown Hotel for her wedding.

FROM THE CROWN TO THE CHURCH is the route also taken for John Elkins' funeral procession in 1909. Maristow Street is behind.

A CROWD celebrating the Coronation of King George V in 1911.

W.H. LAVERTON (the man in the space with the straw hat) joining in the celebrations.

CARNIVAL FLOATS FORMING UP.

DR SHORELAND AND HIS SISTER taking part in the 1906 Carnival.

THE CENTENARY OF THE FOUNDING OF SUNDAY SCHOOLS was celebrated by the Nonconformist churches in Westbury in 1880.

'On Wednesday, July 21st 1880 at two o'clock, the procession started from the West End Chapel, preceded by the band of the Royal Wilts Volunteers and head by the Minister, the Reverend W. Lawrence and the superintendent, Mr Jeffries, and called at the Wesleyan Chapel for the contingent from that school, under the leadership of the Reverend W. Duthie and Mr Barnes: thence up Warminster Street to the Old Congregational Church where it was joined by that School, presided over by the Reverend J. Clarke, B.A., and Mr R. Raikes Taylor; thence to the Upper Meeting where its ranks were augmented by the school under the leadership of the Reverend Amos Bailey and Mr Cusner. It proceeded yet on to Ball's Water where the Schools from Leigh and Marsh, under the care of the Reverends J. Hazzard and W. Finch and led by another band, united with the Westbury Schools and marched through the principal streets to the Market Place where the National Anthem and several pieces were sung by the united schools and a photograph was taken. The procession then repaired to the field, led by the bands, and under the direction of Mr W. Keates, who was captain for the day, refreshments were provided, and games of every description were entered into.'

In 1880 a long exposure would have been necessary to capture the scene, as can be seen from the blurred images of the many people who moved while the photograph was being taken.

A SUNDAY SCHOOL OUTING in nearby Frogmore Fields.

A CHEMIST SHOP in the Market Place, 1922, where the newsagent is now. Mrs Hallam is standing in the doorway.

WYATT'S IRONMONGERS (now Wessex Books and Prints) decorated for Queen Victoria's Diamond Jubilee in 1897.

MRS WYATT. The original, badly-damaged photograph and, on the right, the picture after reconstruction with 'new' hands, book, table, skirt and background. It was fortunate that the face was unaffected!

WYATT'S displaying its line in dustbins and buckets.

THE BALCONY was used for election speeches.

THE TROWBRIDGE CO-OP opened in Westbury on 3 July 1909. A procession of decorated vehicles followed a public tea. After two years the society was pleased to record that 'the sales reach £150 weekly'.

THE ENLARGED CO-OP in 1937. It closed completely in 1987.

From the Market Place

Fore Street, Heywood House
West End, Maristow Street.

The roads radiating from the Market Place will be explored in turn. The aerial photograph of 1956 overleaf, with the map on page 37, will help to orientate you.

The names of many roads have changed over the years. Fore Street was just Turnpike, though, illogically, the toll road must have begun where Fore Street ended. West End was Cheap Street and, before that, Broad Street, while Maristow Street has always been so named.

Off the Trowbridge Road beyond Fore Street is Heywood House built in the Jacobean style in 1869. It was the home of Henry Ludlow Lopes who became Baron Ludlow of Heywood (hence the Ludlow Arms in Fore Street). An earlier house on the site was owned by William Phipps, at one time Governor of Bombay, and the map of 1773 states that a Thomas Phipps owned the house. Other branches of the Phipps family owned property in the town, as will be seen later.

Where Maristow Street leads off from the Market Place by Cannon Green, No. 3, on the left, was the Manor House owned by Sir Mannasseh Massey Lopes who bought the Manor of Westbury from the Earl of Abingdon in 1800. The Lopes Arms changed its allegiance at the same time! Part of the house is now a hat shop.

AN AERIAL PHOTOGRAPH OF WESTBURY taken in 1956. The large house on the left was demolished when the High Street was built in 1965. On the facing page, the street names are given to assist in locating the views that follow.

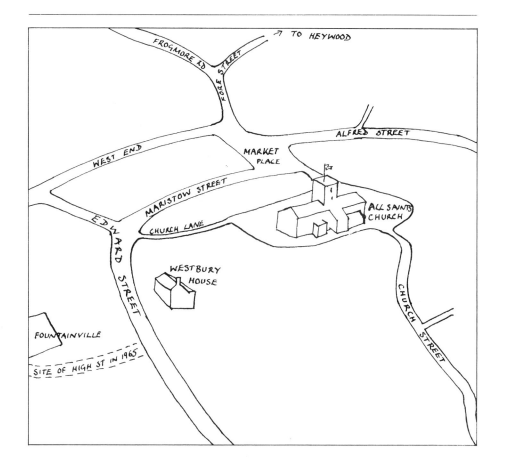

FORE STREET, WESTBURY

THE LUDLOW ARMS, on the right, now has only two storeys. At the old Gas Company cottages in the background the road forks —right to Heywood and Trowbridge, left to Frogmore.

MR DICKS in the doorway of his basket-ware shop in Fore Street. It was about level with the horse and cart on the right in the above photograph.

A.L. JEFFERIES (GLOVER) LTD. in Fore Street. Dormer windows have been added since the picture opposite was taken.

THE CUTTING SHOP OF A.L. JEFFERIES in 1931. Stanley Ingram is fourth from the left and Mr Mead is fifth.

HEYWOOD HOUSE. The Jacobean-style house was built in 1869. However, there was an earlier house on the site.

THE GATES AND LODGE of Heywood House.

WEST END lies in the opposite direction from Fore Street.

LOOKING BACK TO THE MARKET PLACE. Compare the Ludlow Arms behind the car with the photograph on page 38.

Grocery Warehouse,
WEST END, WESTBURY.

STEPHEN BROWN desires to tender his sincere thanks to his friends and supporters generally for their liberal patronage to him for the past 32 years, and begs to intimate that he has taken his Son, JOSEPH BROWN, into Partnership with him, and from this time the Business will be carried on under the name of S. BROWN & SON.

S. BROWN & SON, TEA-DEALERS, BAKERS, and GENERAL FAMILY GROCERS, trust by strict attention to Business, to gain that confidence for the Firm under its new name, which it has received in the past.

December 1st., 1876.

SHOPS SEEM TO CHANGE HANDS FREQUENTLY in Westbury these days. Stephen Brown steadily expanded his business over many years.

THE SON, JOSEPH, WITH HIS SON.

THE SHOP THEN BECAME THE WEST END GROCERY AND PROVISION STORES in the new shop next door. The window display is impressive.

A CARNIVAL FLOAT in front of the old grocery shop.

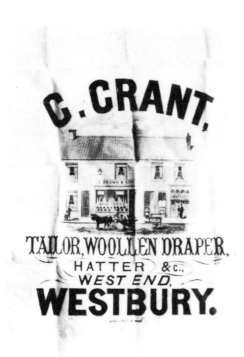

THE SECOND SHOP-FRONT OF S. BROWN &
SON (on the right in this picture) had
been C. Grant's tailors shop.

44

A CARNIVAL FLOAT by the Westbury Mineral Water Co. off West End.

THE DERELICT MINERAL WATER FACTORY before demolition.

THE PILLARED DOORWAY on the left was the entrance to the Georgian Manor House.

GEORGE NICHOLS still decorates his shop (and himself) on national occasions. Here is the 1953 display for the Queen's Coronation. A triumphal arch bridged Maristow Street.

MR WATTS at the entrance to his shop.

MARISTOW STREET from the Edward Street end with J. Bull the butcher on the right. It is difficult to date this picture because the lady in the centre is in a Victorian-style dress, whereas the lady by the shop is wearing a dress of a much later style and the bicycle on the left has pneumatic tyres.

A PICTURE TAKEN FROM A CRUDELY TINTED POSTCARD. The police station was in the building on the right of this picture until 1938. The lower part of Edward Street (formerly Brook Street) bears off to the left. The house in the background is at the beginning of Maristow Street. Church Lane goes off to the foreground right.

SECTION FOUR

From the Market Place

Church Lane, Church Street, Alfred Street

This section covers the remaining roads leading out of the Market Place and the adjoining churchyard.

Round the corner from Maristow Street, past the old police station, is Church Lane, leading back into the churchyard and passing the school which is now the Parish Hall. Mrs S.E. Clayton, who lived in 2 Alfred Street, told Dr Ross her memories of life in 1892 when she was a child. There were two teachers in the school at this time, with one class. Hours were from 9–12 and 2–4 and children started school at the age of 5. Each child took 1d. ($\frac{1}{2}$p) per week to help pay for the upkeep of the school. The cane was frequently used. No dinners or milk were given at school. Homework was given and slates and chalk were taken home to practise writing, arithmetic, etc.

Children played with hoops, spinning tops and marbles. In their spare time they picked peas, potatoes and apples (2s. (10p) per tree picked) or ears of corn at harvest time. They were also employed to scare birds away from crops by hitting pieces of bone together.

An alley from the churchyard leads into Church Street. After that we will return through the churchyard into the Market Place to turn right past the Town Hall into Alfred Street, formerly called Duck Street. I do not know the origin of the names but Alfred Street points to the White Horse and the earthworks of Bratton Castle, the site of Alfred's victory over the Danes in 878AD. As for 'Duck Street', your guess is as good as mine.

A CHILDREN'S CARNIVAL FLOAT in Church Lane. The churchyard is beyond.

A SUNFLOWER FLOAT in the churchyard. Sisters Miss Elliot and Mrs Arnold are standing on the left.

CHILDREN of 1900 in the school built in 1873. It is now the Parish Hall.

WESTBURY CARNIVAL 1919. The girls from left to right are: Alice Cornish, Iris Barber, Phyllis Applegate, Nancy Osbourne, Doris Barber.

Professor E. BLEZARD. *Instructor.* J. S. MILLAR. *Half Back.* E. PIGOTT, Captain. *Left Back.* H. L. JEFFERIES.

H. J. RAINS. *Right Forward.* W. J. RAINS. *Right Back.* C. W. WATTS. *Centre Forward.* L. NUTT. *Goal.* H. NUTT. *Left Forward.*

Westbury Water Polo Team, 1898.

WESTBURY WATER POLO TEAM, 1898.

CHURCH STREET, with the Public Baths built by W.H. Laverton and presented to the town in 1887. The pool was refurbished by the West Wiltshire District Council in 1984.

SOLDIERS OUTSIDE THE BATHS during the First World War.

MISS FRANCIS (who became Mrs E. Webb) standing by the cart. Miss Betty Hobbs (later to become Mrs G. Imber) is standing in front of the barrel-organ ready for the carnival procession.

IN CHURCH STREET AGAIN with the barrel-organ, this time for the Westbury Hospital Carnival. Miss D. Francis (later to become Mrs Argent) is on the left of the group of girls.

A FIRE destroyed many titles, deeds and documents in the offices of Pinniger Finch, the solicitors in Church Street, in February 1935. On the right the Chief Officer C. Fry and Mr S. Collier throw out a burned deed box. Below, H. Pinchen, S. Collier and others search through the charred remains. The Town Seal was also destroyed in the fire.

52371. From Church Tower to White Horse, Westbury

LOOKING ACROSS ALFRED STREET to the White Horse. What was then the vicarage is on the left. Dutch Elm disease in the 1970s denuded the landscape and housing estates now fill the middle distance.

LOOKING UP ALFRED STREET towards the entrance to Bitham Mill.

SECTION FIVE

Cloth Mills

Bitham Mill, Angel Mill

Westbury had been an important cloth-making town since medieval times, its prosperity evinced by its fine church. This trade declined in the seventeenth century. Around 1800 several mills were built in the area, including three close to the church.

Of these three, Bitham Mill off Alfred Street, Angel Mill in the corner between Church Street and Edward Street and The Town Mill at the bottom of Alfred Street close to the Market Place, only the first two remain, though not as mills. The Town Mill, owned by William Matravers, burned down in 1861.

Angel Mill is notable for being one of the first to be powered by steam. Matravers and Overbury installed a 20hp Boulton and Watt steam engine in 1818. The fortunes of the mills, despite the innovations, steadily declined. In 1849, both Bitham and Angel Mills were bought by Abraham Laverton who started a revival in the cloth trade with the Laverton Cloth Company. He and his son W.H. Laverton, to whom he had handed over the business in 1880, became benefactors to the town and their names will continue to be mentioned in later sections.

The Angel Mill was the last to close, in 1967, and the future of the building is still in contention as it steadily decays. The Bitham Mill was in use as a factory for surgical beds and appliances until 1988 and is likely to be developed for residential use, while retaining its character.

The wages for women in the Laverton Mills in 1892 were 6s. (30p) per week. Hours of work were 6 a.m. to 6 p.m. To put this into perspective, bread was then 4d. (2p) a loaf, eggs 1s. (5p) for 28 (why 28 I wonder?) and a woman's dress was about 4s.11d. (25p).

FACTORY, WESTBURY.

THE ENTRANCE TO BITHAM MILL in 1921.

EXTENDING THE BITHAM MILL CHIMNEY in the 1920s.

BITHAM MILL WORKERS in 1919: John Crook, Alan Player, Fanny Jefferies, J. Rowe, George Styles.

THE SPINNING SHOP, Bitham Mill.

THE MILL POND OF BITHAM MILL looks very different today as a sunken garden at the edge of the churchyard.

THE FACTORY WHISTLE from Angel Mill must have been a familiar sound to the people of Westbury.

THE CEILINGS WERE VERY LOW in parts of Angel Mill, as this maintenance workshop view shows.

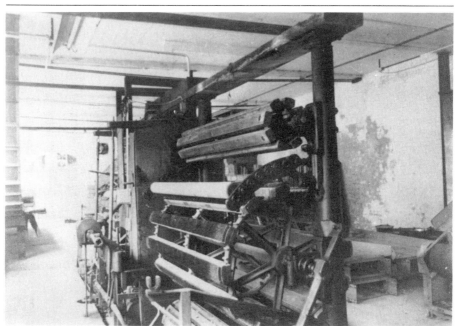

AN UPRIGHT GIG for raising the nap in Angel Mill.

A CHEESE-WINDING MACHINE.

A STORE ROOM in Angel Mill.

A DELIVERY BICYCLE.

A WARPING MACHINE made by Hollingsworth & Co. Ltd., Atlas Works, Huddersfield, in 1891.

CLOTH-PRESSING MACHINES.

Edward Street

Were our great-grandparents to follow our tour in reverse – that is, viewing today's town from the past – they would so far have not felt too lost or uncomfortable (providing they did not try to park their carts!).

For much of the rest of the route, time has dealt less kindly with the urban scene, though there are still many links with the past.

Edward Street certainly has changed because the new, 1965, High Street opens from it. The lower part of Edward Street, where it joins West End to Maristow Street, was previously known as Brook Street.

AN AERIAL PHOTOGRAPH from 1983.

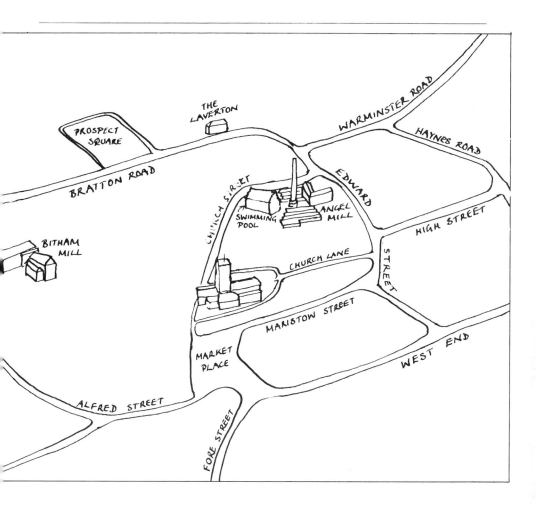

KENDRICK'S GARAGE in 1929. Mr Boffey and Alan Kendrick are in the centre and Mr Grist is on the left.

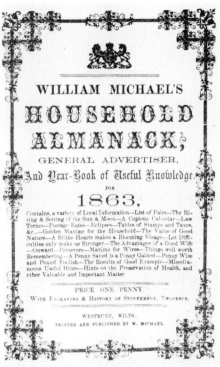

WILLIAM MICHAEL established a printing business in 1858 in the room above the shop illustrated below. The cover of his *Household Almanack* is shown here. Michael's *Advertising Sheets* over the years tell us a lot about the businesses of Westbury and examples appear throughout this book. The business was bought by A.E. & H. Holloway in 1911 and only closed a few years ago. The shop-front below is decorated for the Coronation of 1937.

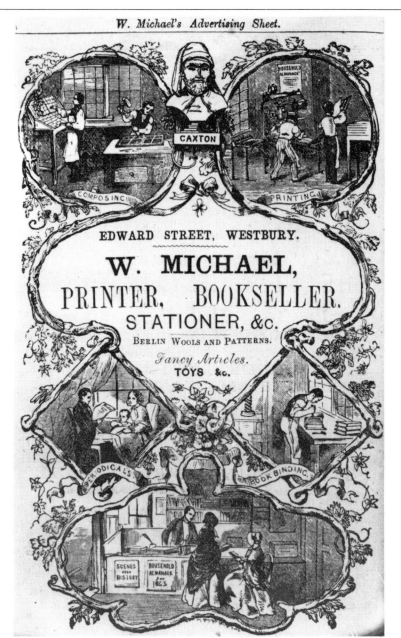

AN INTERESTING COVER to W. Michael's *Advertising Sheet.*

THE HARDWARE SHOP of W.J. Ford – it must have been hard work to take the stock in when it rained.

THE SAME SHOP after being taken over by C. Rogers & Co. It is still a hardware store under the name of G.L. & D.M. Davies Ltd.

WESTBURY POST OFFICE STAFF in 1902. The present post office is on the same site – 26 Edward Street.

A VIEW OF THE DERELICT FONTENVILLE in 1959 (sometimes written as Fontainevilla or Fountainville), before demolition in 1961 to make way for the High Street car-park. Mr J.J. Singer lived there in 1867 and Mrs Browne in 1899.

THE AMATEUR DRAMATIC SOCIETY CAST in front of Fontenville.

PLAYERS IN CHARLES DICKENS' *A Christmas Carol*. Mr James Francis is wearing the top hat.

A REAR VIEW OF WESTBURY HOUSE. This house has changed little, externally, since it was taken over to house the County Public Library in 1970. The library had previously been in the Old Town Hall.

INTERIOR VIEWS OF WESTBURY HOUSE, taken in 1922.

THE WALL TO THE LEFT OF THIS LADY SHOPPER is that of Westbury House and, to the right, that of Fontenville – where the High Street is now. The picture below shows the High Street being built in 1965.

BILL SAY, Stan Hillman, Fred Taylor and Alfred Taylor in 1920.

THE ONLY PETROL PUMP IN WESTBURY in 1921. Its site was near the present supermarket. Mr Harry Taylor and Mrs Fred Taylor are in the picture.

THE ORIGINAL SHOP OF RAINES THE BAKERS, since demolished, is on the right. They have now moved further up the road.

THOUGH NOT IN EDWARD STREET, this float is by Parsons and Raines, Caterers.

THIS CARD IS TITLED 'WARMINSTER ROAD', but the view is *from* there, looking down Edward Street to the Angel Inn. The Capital and Counties Bank (now Lloyds) is beyond the shop.

A CARNIVAL PROCESSION passing H.C. Cousens & Co., Drapers.

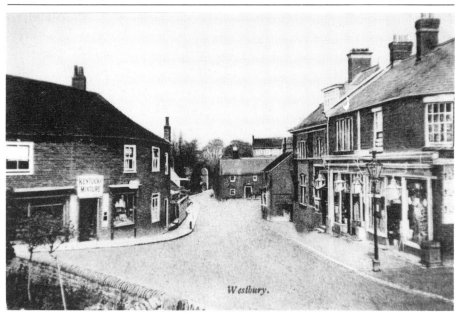

EDWARD STREET FROM BRATTON ROAD. The end of Angel Mill can be seen in the background. From a tinted postcard.

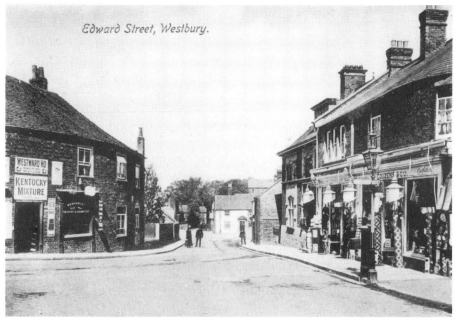

NOTE THE ARRIVAL OF A PILLAR-BOX and the lamppost doubling up as a signpost.

THE LITTLE GIRLS on the right add charm to the picture. It is a pity more of Angel Mill is not visible behind the Angel Pub. This was an old and badly-damaged picture.

LOOKING UP EDWARD STREET to the infants school on Bratton Road. The sign-board on the right points 'to the bath' in Church Street.

THE CENTRE OF ATTENTION is not known but it would seem to be giving off steam or smoke. Note the gentleman with the bicycle who we will meet again.

Bratton Road and the White Horse

The road bends round the base of the scarp below the chalk figure (now cement faced) and, as both feature in many of the views, they are combined in one section.

Turning left from the top of Edward Street brings one into Bratton Road which was claimed to be 'a most healthy part of Westbury' in the Belle Vue College advertisement. A good view is implied in the name of the college as well! Certainly the road is considerably elevated above the rest of the town but whether the drains below were bad or it was damp which made the rest of the town less healthy, history does not relate.

More evidence of the public-spirited works of the Lavertons may be seen in the Laverton Institute and Prospect Square.

The White Horse has been the subject of much discussion as to its antiquity and purpose. Popular tradition has it that it was cut to commemorate Alfred's victory over the Danes nearby at Ethandun in 878 AD and their final surrender, two weeks later, at the Iron Age earthworks of Bratton Castle. There is no evidence to support this and the earliest figure appeared in around 1700. This was a smaller strange beast facing the other way. The steward of the Earl of Abingdon arranged for the present horse to be cut in 1778, obliterating the original, but received no thanks for his pains, the horse being described as a 'miserable creature'. It has been cleaned, tidied and refaced several times since.

Despite the evidence, the more romantic link with Alfred is perpetuated still in well-known guide books of England and the source for this is not difficult to find. Many postcards, until recently, printed the story under the picture and an example appears in this section.

WESTBURY INFANTS' SCHOOL built in 1883 in Bratton Road, opposite Edward Street.

NO. 6 BRATTON ROAD – probably the oldest dwelling in Westbury, built at the beginning of the seventeenth century.

ON THE BEND, as one turns out of Edward Street into Bratton Road, was the cycle shop of J. Martingate, also motor agents. 1906.

ODDFELLOWS HALL.

W.H. LAVERTON in the uniform of Lord Lieutenant of Wiltshire. The Laverton Institute, opposite, was built by his father, Abraham Laverton, for the town in 1873. The attractively-designed group of workers' houses, a little further up Bratton Road at Prospect Square, were also built by him.

THE LAVERTON INSTITUTE is now the Town Hall and lacks its clock 'tower'. These photographs were taken in 1906.

THE SHOP NEXT TO THE LAVERTON WAS BAINES – Ladies' Outfitters.

A WEDDING PARTY leaving the Laverton. The entrance into Prospect Square can be seen beyond the car on the right.

MOUNTED TROOPS in Bratton Road in 1914.

BELLE VUE COLLEGE was opposite the Laverton Institute. The healthy situation of Bratton Road claimed in the advertisement makes it an ideal choice of location for the Cemetery shown below! The superintendent living in the lodge in 1899 was called Albin Randall, though he was not related to the author. A George Randall was mayor of Westbury in 1768, 1775 and 1781.

TRAVELLERS ON THE BRATTON ROAD — the Misses Bailey from Alfred Street.

A MAN AND BOY WITH A FARM CART.

DRIVING SHEEP.

SHEPHERDS WITH THEIR SHEEP. There is much erosion around the feet of the White Horse in the picture above. It had been cleaned and remodelled in 1872. The picture below is from a tinted postcard of 1905.

WESTBURY WHITE HORSE

Westbury White Horse and Neighbourhood.
From the Iron Works.

A NINETEENTH-CENTURY ENGRAVING, in fact from the station rather than the Iron Works.

THE EARTHWORKS OF BRATTON CASTLE are clearly shown in this aerial view.

SILVER JUBILEE
·1910 - 1935

Illustrated Souvenir

OF THE

BONFIRE

Erected by the Boy Scouts of Westbury and Bratton near the Westbury White Horse, and ignited by J. S. MARKS, ESQ., J.P. at 10 p.m. on Monday, May 6, 1935.

Price 3d.

Proceeds for Scout Funds.

A BONFIRE, consisting of a 30ft. pile of wood and old tyres, was to be one of a chain of beacons set up to celebrate the Silver Jubilee of King George V. 'The roar of 60ft. sheet of flame almost drowned the words of dedication – In honour of his Majesty King George the Fifth.'

94

THE WEST OF ENGLAND RAMBLERS' FEDERATION, 26 June 1937.

RAMBLERS by the head of the White Horse.

SHEEP PENNED BELOW THE WHITE HORSE. A sheep fair was held annually on the Downs on the first Tuesday of September.

THE HORSE-DRAWN REAPER. The sheaves were stacked into stooks by hand. The elm trees were characteristic of the landscape below the edge of the Plain until Dutch Elm disease struck.

Westbury White Horse. This picturesque memorial of Alfred the Great's decisive victory over the Danes at Ethandunes (Edington) A.D. 878, is situated about two miles from the town of Westbury. It was formed by stripping the turf from the chalk downs on the northern slope of Salisbury Plain. The extreme length of the Horse from head to tail, both included 175 feet. Height from feet to shoulder, 107 feet. Circumference of eye 25 feet.

STACKING SHEAVES INTO RICKS.

THRESHING BY STEAM.

THE MILITARY have long been associated with Salisbury Plain. This is an impressive camp cooker.

THE WESTBURY TERRITORIALS' COOK STAFF, 1905.

SECTION EIGHT

Warminster Road

Warminster Road also begins where Bratton Road began. It is built up to the outskirts of the town, except for the break through the cutting where Leighton Park straddles the road. This section stops short before Leighton Park which, with Chalford, is the subject of Section Nine.

Town End was the name given to the area where Leigh (previously Lower) Road turns off the Warminster Road opposite Hospital Road (Dowdens Lane) but it has little relevance now.

WARMINSTER ROAD between Haynes Road and Edward Street with the sixteenth-century/ seventeenth-century thatched house before it was demolished in around 1909.

Westbury

THE SAME VIEW LATER with the red brick replacement shop. It is still a butchers shop today.

BULL'S THE BUTCHERS' DISPLAY outside the thatched house.

THE HOUSE OVER A.H. EDIS' GREENGROCER SHOP is still being built at the Bratton Road end of Warminster Road in 1926.

Warminster Road, Westbury.

THE "VINEYARDS,"

WESTBURY, WILTS.

Establishment for Young Ladies.

Conducted by

MISS PREECE.

❖ Terms and References on Application. ❖

NOW HEADING IN THE WARMINSTER DIRECTION, this was the view from the top of Haynes Road. The 'Vineyards' Establishment for Young Ladies was the first house on the right.

HOUSES NEXT TO THE FUTURE SITE OF THE CINEMA, well before they were demolished in 1921. Another three-wheeled 'velocipede' is in the foreground.

DR SHORELAND AND HIS WIFE with a donkey cart in 1905, by the gardens where the Vista Cinema was later built.

THE VISTA CINEMA, here shown almost complete in 1922, was destroyed by fire in 1988.

THE CINEMA IN ITS HEYDAY in the mid-1930s.

TWO VIEWS of the town end of Warminster Road taken some years apart.

LAYING THE FOUNDATION STONE CEREMONY, 1930, for the Cottage Hospital above Nightingale Hill which was then known as Hospital Hill. Hospital Road was previously Dowdens Lane. On the dais are: Revd Antrobus, Mr Seward (treasurer) Revd Alexander (in the surplice), Mrs Pinniger, Lady Sybil Phipps (standing), W.H. Laverton, Matron Howells, Mr Hayward, Mr Percy Pepler. To the right are Mr Hart (verger) and Mr Cutler.

A LONG VIEW back up Warminster Road with the church in the background.

THE ORIGINAL WESLEYAN CHAPEL, built in 1809, became known as the Upper Congregational Chapel. It was later used as a Masonic Hall but has now been disused for several years.

THE FUNERAL PROCESSION OF MR R.R. TAYLOR in 1908 moving down Warminster Road. He had been the Sunday School Superintendent of the Congregational Church for many years and owned a photographic studio in Warminster Road.

Warminster Road, Westbury.

TOWN END where Leigh Road (Lower Road) goes off to the left and the end of Hospital Road can be seen on the right. Mead's Brewery is in the centre, behind Ye Oak Inn. From Tills Letter Card.

FIRST PRIZE WINNERS, 'HARVESTERS', in the 1913 Westbury Hospital Carnival.

THE 'LEST YE FORGET' BARREL-ORGAN turns up again in 1912, outside Tills photographic studio. It was probably Taylor's before him. The gentleman on the left in a top hat is Mr Cutler.

CHARLES BAILEY, the blind Bandmaster, leading the carnival procession. His friend and Band Sergeant, John Elkins, guided him from behind (here not very successfully it would seem!). William Elkins is next to his father on the left (not playing, perhaps to tell Mr Bailey to bear left).

ANOTHER LONG VIEW DOWN THE ROAD.

A FAIRGROUND STEAM LORRY, towing two caravans, runs off the road. Could the spectator with the bike be the same chap we met in Edward Street?

Leighton House, Chalford and Leigh Road

The lease of Leighton Park was acquired by the Phipps brothers, Nicholas and Henry, in 1585. It encompassed a larger area then and there were two large houses. A descendant, Thomas Henry Hele Phipps, inherited the estate and built the present Leighton House in 1800.

William Henry Laverton, with whom you are already familiar, bought the estate in 1888 and enlarged the house. He had a private theatre built in the grounds, in which Dame Melba and Caruso performed. A bridge, leading to the stable block, was erected over the cutting for the Warminster Road. He also had a cricket pitch laid and an annual match was played between the Australians and W.H. Laverton's XI. In 1890, Dr W.G. Grace played and the Australians were soundly beaten.

In 1921 the house and park were sold to become a private school – Victoria College. It closed in 1936 and remained empty until the War Office requisitioned it for a Convalescent Depot in 1939. It took over responsibility for the selection of officers after the war and then for the selection of National Service Officers. It was in 1949 that it assumed its present title of Regular Commissions Board and I was one of its candidates soon after, breaking my wrist in the process.

Chalford was a separate hamlet in the hollow beyond the Park on the Warminster Road where Laverton Road joins it. It is now on the outskirts of Westbury.

Leigh Road follows the perimeter wall of the Park on the west side so it is included in this section and links Sections Eight and Ten.

THE LENGTH OF WESTBURY, from Westbury Leigh to the cement works, in 1983.

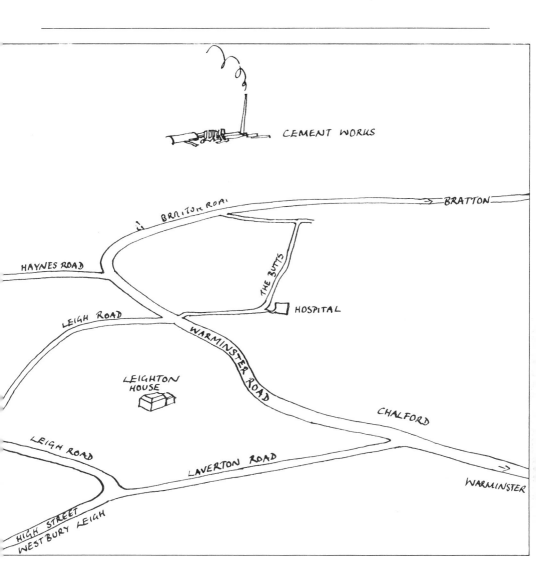

CEMENT WORKS

BRATTON

BRATTON ROAD

HAYNES ROAD

THE BUTTS

HOSPITAL

LEIGH ROAD

WARMINSTER ROAD

LEIGHTON HOUSE

CHALFORD

LEIGH ROAD

LAVERTON ROAD

WARMINSTER

HIGH STREET
WESTBURY LEIGH

LEIGHTON HOUSE built by Thomas Phipps in 1800.

THE HOUSE WAS BOUGHT BY WILLIAM LAVERTON in 1888 and then enlarged.

LEIGHTON PARK showing house and lodge.

THE PRIVATE THEATRE built off Leighton Lane in the Park. At the time of this photograph (after 1921) it was the speech hall of Victoria College.

WESTBURY COMRADES' FÊTE held on the Leighton Sports Ground.

A CEDAR TREE 60ft. high was struck by lightning on 3 August 1904 in Leighton Park.

USH.   W GREENLAND.   R. FIELD   I.H. NEWTON.   F.H. GRIFFIN   F.C. FRY.
(Steward)

G. A. BARRETT.   F. S. WYATT.   W.H. LAVERTON. Esq. DL., JP., CC.   H. CLAYTON   H.E. TILL
(Hon Treasurer)   (Vice-Chairman)   (President)   (Hon. Secretary)   (Asst. Secretary)

THE FOUNDERS OF WESTBURY COMRADES' CLUB outside Leighton House, the home of Mr W.H. Laverton, in 1920. Mr H.E. Till, on the right of the front row, was a photographer in Westbury and several of his postcards and photographs are reproduced in this book.

THE BRIDGE TO THE STABLES in Leighton Park. When Warminster Road was widened in 1976 a new bridge had to be built.

THE ROAD FROM CHALFORD to the bridge.

A PAINTING OF THE BELL INN, Chalford, by A. Webb, 1930.

ALL THE INHABITANTS OF CHALFORD seem to have been assembled for this photograph. It would be a very dangerous place to stand today.

Chalford Westbury.

A FAMILY BY THE BELL INN, Chalford, in 1915.

THE TOLL-HOUSE on the Warminster Road which survived until 1960. Turnpikes were taken down and burned in 1872, having been in use since 1769.

WESTBURY SENIOR SCHOOL, built in 1844 on Leigh Road. It is still in use though much altered.

THERE WAS AN INDIGO FACTORY off the Leigh Road. Indigo Lane survives as a memory after the factory's demolition in the 1970s.

A DECORATED HOUSE in Leigh Road, but for what?

LEIGH ROAD with the wall of Leighton Park.

SECTION TEN

Westbury Leigh

Having reached the bottom of Leigh Road we can turn right into Westbury Leigh. This has grown up astride the narrow Frome road, now totally inadequate for the heavy lorries that continually squeeze their way through.

The cloth industry gave way to leather with a tannery and glove factories. The main mill building, of what became Boulton's Glove Factory, is still used and the mill pond remains.

Being part of the Parish of Westbury, the Church of the Holy Saviour built in 1876 on a site given by Mr Leconby Phipps of Leighton House, is officially described as a Chapel of Ease. Mrs R.L.H. Phipps paid for the tower, which was added in 1889, as a memorial to her husband. It is a well-proportioned building.

There was active non-conformist worship in the area, particularly in Westbury Leigh. A branch from the Southwick Baptist Church was established in 1662. The congregation moved to a barn on the site of the present chapel. The barn was converted into a meeting house and the larger chapel was built in 1796. The secession in 1810 of the then pastor and supporters to form the Penknap chapel is mentioned later in this section.

From Tower Hill by Penknap we go on for a brief glimpse at Chalcot House, which, happily, was rescued from dereliction in 1971 by the present owner. Then, finally, down to the delightful little church in Old Dilton.

SCOTT'S BAKERS SHOP.

THE BOY WITH THE CART has grown up since the previous picture and telephone wires have come to Westbury Leigh.

SCOTT'S SHOP was destroyed by fire in the 1930s.

LOOKING TOWARDS BALLSWATER.

TWO VIEWS OF WESTBURY LEIGH looking towards Leighton House on the hill.

H.F. BARBER'S SHOP AND BAKERY.

LOOKING WEST with an assembly of children.

Glove Factory, Westbury Leigh.

Glove Factory, Westbury Leigh

BOULTON'S GLOVE FACTORY, 1905. It was closed in 1950 though part of the building continues to be in use.

Glove Factory. Westbury Leigh.

VIEW FROM THE SCHOOL.

THE TANNERY.

CHURCH OF THE HOLY SAVIOUR. Westbury Leigh. Building began in 1876 and the tower was added in 1889.

A FAMILY outside the Phipps Arms.

THE PHIPPS ARMS.

WESTBURY LEIGH BAPTIST CHURCH is visible from The Apple Tree in the Westbury direction. Another woolly tradition is kept alive on this card.

AFTER THE SECOND WORLD WAR, The Apple Tree became a residence. Originally, it was a grist or fulling mill. The Biss Brook runs alongside. The house is about 400 years old and the stone frontage was added in 1750.

THE MAN LOOKING INTO THE BISS BROOK (right) would seem to have been painted in for artistic effect. Beyond The Apple Tree in this direction is Penknap Providence Chapel (below). It was built in 17 weeks in 1810 on a site given by Mr Stephen Applegate. During this time, services were held in the open and it never rained – hence 'Providence' Chapel. The reason it is so close to the Westbury Leigh Baptist Church was because the Baptist Minister was suspected of having Wesleyan leanings, so he and 23 followers left to form Penknap.

PENKNAP CHAPEL

TOWER HILL, WESTBURY LEIGH.

DILTON MARSH HALT is to the right of this picture on the GWR line from Westbury to Salisbury.

A MILE OR SO AFTER GOING THROUGH THE BRIDGE at Tower Hill, on the Frome Road, lies Chalcot House on high ground commanding excellent views. It dates from 1541 and was the home of another Phipps, Paul. The Palladian front, inspired by Inigo Jones, was added around 1680. This photograph was taken in 1911.

BEFORE REACHING CHALCOT and off to the left, is Dilton, still part (tything) of the Parish of Westbury. The Phipps family owned considerable property here. There were two large Cloth Mills and a Grist Mill supplied by the Biss which rises nearby. The Church of St Mary is fifteenth century and on the site of one dating from the twelfth or thirteenth century. Though closed since 1900 it is well maintained and two services a year are held – Harvest Thanksgiving and a Candlelit Advent Carol Service with the joint choir of All Saints and Holy Saviour. Inside is a three-decker pulpit, box pews and musicians' gallery. Dilton is referred to as Old Dilton to differentiate from Dilton Marsh which is now a large village and parish in its own right.

Haynes Road

Westbourne Lane, Station Road,
The Ham

Now we must jump back into the centre of Westbury to go north-west from Warminster Road, down Haynes Road (Lane) and on up Station Road to The Ham on a crest beyond the railway.

Had we been travellers in 1800, long before the railway was built, our route to The Ham would have sounded more interesting. From Perry Way via Small Bridge and Grass Acres Road, Oldfield Road (as it now is) was reached. There one crossed Tadpole Bridge, Tyning and Cowards Withy before climbing Ham Slope to join Storridge Road and Brook Farm Road.

The railway and the ironworks up by The Ham are the subject of the final section.

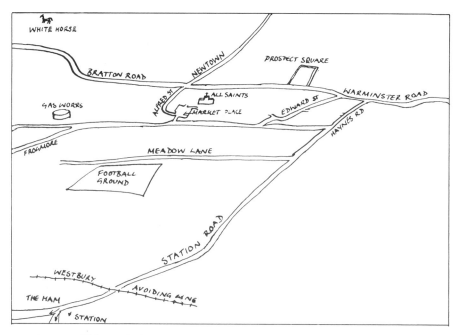

MAP from a 1983 aerial photograph.

THE CARNIVAL forming up in Haynes Lane. West End is in the background.

HAYNES ROAD from the start of Station Road.

THE HOSPITAL IN WESTBOURNE ROAD built to commemorate Queen Victoria's Diamond Jubilee in 1897. The end facing us was extended a few years later. Angel Mill is in the background.

TWO EARLY VIEWS of Station Road.

Station Road, Westbury.

WESTBURY UNITED FOOTBALL CLUB.
1921-22.

F. Weston.   E. H. Arnold.   F. Angel.   R. Porter.   S. Collier.   C. W. D. Ward.   T. Hartshorn.   L. Webb.   W. Scott.
(Committee)   *(Chairman)*   *(Asst. Trainer)*   *(Capt.)*   *(Vice-Chair)*   *(Hon. Sec.)*   *(Team Manager)*

A. Alford *(Committee)*.   W. Wheeler.   S. Griffin.   C. Dunning.   G. Benham *(Trainer)*.

F. Porter.   S. Ferris.   G. Clinch.   E. Long.   S. Preston.

THE FOOTBALL GROUND is in Meadow Lane off Station Road.

THE WESTBURY GLOVE CO. LTD. factory built in 1908 and closed in 1960.

IN THE FACTORY.

A LORRY IN TROUBLE in Station Road. The Railway Inn is in the background.

THE CHEDLET CHEESE FACTORY is top left and The Ham is on the right. Middle left is the iron works and in the centre is the station showing the island platforms. The road over the railway is Station Road joining Storridge Road at The Ham.

CHEDLET CHEESE FACTORY on The Ham. It was a RAF depot at the end of the First World War.

MR DENMAN is in the back of the van loading boxes.

LT. FLINT WAS FLYING A BRISTOL FIGHTER FROM OLD SARUM, accompanied by Lt. Brennan, both of the Kings' Own Regiment, in 1923. They lost their bearings and flew low hoping to read the railway station name boards. Running short of fuel, they tried to land but hit the chimney of The Cedars on The Ham (the present home of the author). The plane crashed into the minehole at the bottom of the next-door neighbour's garden which was contaminated by sewage. Mr Bradbury and another neighbour, Mr Owen, assisted the officers out of the foul water. They suffered no broken bones but had swallowed much of the water and were taken to the hospital by a car from Taylor's Garage, after Mrs Bradbury had revived the officers with brandy. Mr Bradbury was allowed to salvage parts of the aircraft which he sold as souvenirs in aid of the Cottage Hospital.

THE CRASHED AIRCRAFT from The Cedars garden.

SECTION TWELVE

Railway and Iron Works

Iron and the railway were linked from their beginnings, for, when digging a cutting for the railway on The Ham in 1841, iron ore was found. The Brunel broad gauge station was opened in 1848 and the Westbury Iron Company was established alongside in 1857. The GWR was a customer for furnace slag and provided transport for the pig-iron and iron oxide produced.

Initially the railway ran from Thingley Junction then was extended to Frome in 1850 and to Warminster a year later. It was not until 1874 that the connection was made with Salisbury. In 1900 a new station was built with two long island platforms, which remain today, and the standard gauge route from London via Lavington was brought in.

In the '20s and '30s the main line to Plymouth and Penzance was known as the Westbury route. The opening of the avoiding line speeded up the journey and slip coaches were dropped before Heywood Junction to be brought into the station.

The iron company carried out smelting. However, the company struggled and was eventually bought out in 1903. The New Westbury Iron Company spent large sums on modernising the plant but, in 1908, they had to stop smelting due to a drop in the price of pig-iron. There was also a demand for iron oxide from gas undertakings that tapered off in 1920, which coincided with a five-week strike that achieved nothing. Only half the workers were reinstated. In March 1922 smelting was restarted but stopped in September. A final attempt in 1923 failed when a hot spot caused the firebricks to disintegrate. The use of slag for tarmacadam road surfacing and the production of iron oxide kept the works going into the 1930s. In 1939 the plant was sold, mainly for scrap which was then in great demand. All that remains are the water-filled ore pits and a wall by the town post office built from furnace slag blocks.

THE GWR STATION built by Brunel at Westbury in 1848 before demolition.

PLATELAYERS AT WESTBURY STATION or possibly a demolition gang.

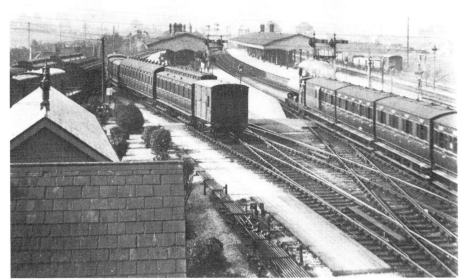

A VIEW OF THE STATION in 1915.

A PHOTOGRAPH FROM THE SAME PERIOD, from a Tills Letter Card, showing the Iron Works.

STATION STAFF.

WESTBURY NORTH SIGNALBOX is in the foreground. The sidings on the right lead into the Iron Works.

WESTBURY STATION STAFF.

RAILWAY AND IRON WORKS.

AN ASLEF BANNER of the 1920s.

AN ASLEF BANNER of the 1920s.

A LOVELY SIGHT – *Windsor Castle* hauling the Royal Train on the avoiding line in 1939.

NOT AT WESTBURY but the fireman, in the cab of the Royal Engine *Britannia* for Queen Victoria's train in 1900, was the grandfather of Mr Tony Hannaford of Westbury.

FROM THE IRON WORKS, over the station we see minehole lake, The Railway Inn and the wooded landscape to the White Horse.

STATION AND IRON WORKS.

GALLOWAY HOUSE being built.

THE BOILERS.

Westbury Iron Works.

THE 'PIG' BED is in the foreground. Galloway House is here complete with a water tank on the roof.

WORKMEN IN THE IRON WORKS. Pay in 1892 was 16s.(80p) per week. Hours of work were 6 a.m. to 6 p.m.

SLAG TRUCKS on the 2ft. gauge track. Galloway House is complete here but without the water tank.

STRIPPING A SLAG POT.

WAGON SHED.

A TWO FOOT GAUGE LOCOMOTIVE made by Peckett in 1898.

STANDARD GAUGE LOCOMOTIVE 0-4-0 made by Andrew Barclay & Son in 1912. This is one of the two bought from Woolwich Arsenal, either *George* or *Neptune*.

ACKNOWLEDGEMENTS

It will have been apparent that this is not the work of a scholar or the fruit of years of painstaking collation of material by a local history society. It is merely an offering back to the town from a photographer who has a large number of copy negatives of old photographs and postcards. These had been brought to me for copying or lent so that exhibitions could be mounted in aid of the church. From the great interest shown in these exhibitions I felt bounden to accede to the request to prepare a book, so that a glimpse of our heritage can be more widely appreciated and be passed on in a compact and lasting form.

There will be omissions and maybe errors for which I apologise in advance but I hope that, as a result, information and previously unseen material will be unearthed so that, one day, a follow-up book can be published.

None of the pictures have come from official archives but from the collections and treasured family photographs of many kind people of Westbury who have lent them for me to copy. Help has come in many ways to make the book possible and it is to everyone who lent their pictures or their memories that I offer my sincere thanks and hope that they will gain as much pleasure as I have in seeing the pictures live again. In naming names I dread missing one off – please forgive me if so.

Many of the photographs lent were themselves copies so I do not know the origins of some, nor in some cases may they be representative of the quality of the original. I hope that I have not unwittingly wronged anyone in the compilation of this book, but if I have I am sorry. It may help to know that any royalties from the book are tithed to the repair fund for All Saints and Holy Saviour churches – our common heritage – for which £77,000 is needed over the next decade for essential repairs alone.

With my fingers crossed for accuracy, I thank the following: Mr V.J. Archard, Miss R.L. Argent, Mr Carpenter, Mr R. Clayton, Mrs T.J. Clements, Mr & Mrs A.H. Hannaford, Mr B.W. Holloway, Mr G.W.W. Laverton, Mr V.J. Linham, Mrs J.H.J. Mantell, Mrs Marks, Mr Michael Marshman, Mr George Nichols, Mr A.B. Poffley, Mrs Ross, Mrs Ivy Scull, Canon M.R. Sinker, Mrs D.J. Smith, Mr H.E. Smith, Mr Turk, Major Robin Wilson.